MUHAMMAD ALI
A TRIBUTE TO THE GREATEST

BOOKS BY THOMAS HAUSER

GENERAL NON-FICTION

Missing

The Trial of Patrolman Thomas Shea

For Our Children (with Frank Macchiarola)

The Family Legal Companion

Final Warning: The Legacy of Chernobyl (with Dr Robert Gale)

Arnold Palmer: A Personal Journey

Confronting America's Moral Crisis (with Frank Macchiarola)

Healing: A Journal of Tolerance and Understanding

With This Ring (with Frank Macchiarola)

A God to Hope For

Thomas Hauser on Sports

Reflections

BOXING NON-FICTION

The Black Lights: Inside the World of Professional Boxing

Muhammad Ali: His Life and Times

Muhammad Ali: Memories

Muhammad Ali: In Perspective

Muhammad Ali & Company

A Beautiful Sickness

A Year at the Fights

Brutal Artistry

The View from Ringside

Chaos, Corruption, Courage, and Glory

I Don't Believe It, But It's True

Knockout (with Vikki LaMotta)

MUHAMMAD ALI

A TRIBUTE TO THE GREATEST

THOMAS HAUSER

SUNDAY TIMES BESTSELLING AUTHOR

HarperSport

An Imprint of HarperCollins*Publishers*

HarperSport
An imprint of HarperCollins*Publishers*
1 London Bridge Street
London SE1 9GF

www.harpercollins.co.uk

Portions of this book were previously published as
The Lost Legacy of Muhammad Ali (Sport Classic Books) and
Muhammad Ali: The Lost Legacy (Robson Books)

First published by HarperCollins*Publishers* 2016

1 3 5 7 9 10 8 6 4 2

A catalogue record of this book is
available from the British Library

ISBN 978-0-00-815244-4

Printed and bound in Great Britain by
Clays Ltd, St Ives plc

AUTHOR'S NOTE

Muhammad Ali: His Life and Times, which was published in 1991, is often referred to as the definitive account of the first fifty years of Ali's life. This is the companion volume to that book. An earlier version was published in the United Kingdom in 2005 under the title *Muhammad Ali: The Lost Legacy*. At that time, it contained all of the essays and articles I'd written about Ali. *Muhammad Ali: A Tribute to the Greatest* contains recently authored pieces, including the previously unpublished essay, 'The Long Sad Goodbye'.

Thomas Hauser

Muhammad Ali belongs to the world.
This book is dedicated to Muhammad
and to everyone who is part of his story.